SCIENCE QUEST

THE SECRET FORMULA

DAN GREEN

QED

Quarto is the authority on a wide range of topics.

Quarto educates, entertains and enriches the lives of our readers—enthusiasts and lovers of hands-on living.

www.quartoknows.com

Cover Design: Mandy Norman
Illustrator: David Shephard
Editor: Amanda Askew
Designer: Punch Bowl Design
QED Project Editor: Ruth Symons
Managing Editor: Victoria Garrard
Design Manager: Anna Lubecka

First published in the UK in 2013 by
QED Publishing
Part of The Quarto Group
The Old Brewery, 6 Blundell Street
London, N7 9BH

A catalogue record for this book is available from the British Library.

ISBN 978 1 78171 700 4
9 8 7 6 5 4 3
HH122019

Printed in China

Picture credits
Shutterstock: Aleksandr Bryliaev, 41; ARENA Creative, 21, 42; Eliks 10; haru,13; Gorbash Varvara, 38; K.A.Willis, 1, 40; mik photographer, 5, 12, 18, 33, 39; Mitar Vidakovic, 2, 21, 26; olavs, 31; oriontrail, 43; PhotostockAR, 31, 48; Shcherbakov Roman, 37; Takra, 22; Zora Rossi, 23

How to begin your adventure

Are you ready for an amazing adventure that will test your brainpower to the limit – full of mind-bending puzzles, twists and turns? Then this is the book for you!

The Secret Formula is no ordinary book – you don't read the pages in order, 1, 2, 3... Instead you jump forwards and backwards through the book as the plot unfolds. Sometimes you may lose your way, but the story will soon guide you back to where you need to be.

The story starts on page 4. Straight away, there are puzzles to solve, choices to make and clues to pick up. The choices will look something like this:

IF YOU THINK THE
CORRECT ANSWER IS A,
GO TO PAGE 10

IF YOU THINK THE
CORRECT ANSWER IS B,
GO TO PAGE 18

Your task is to solve each problem. So, if you think the correct answer is A, turn to page 10 and look for the same symbol in blue. That's where you will find the next part of the story.

If you make the wrong choice, the text will explain where you went wrong and let you have another go.

The problems in this adventure are about matter, materials and chemical reactions. To solve them you must use your science skills. To help you, there's a glossary of useful words at the back of the book, starting on page 44.

ARE YOU READY?
TURN THE PAGE AND LET YOUR ADVENTURE BEGIN!

THE SECRET FORMULA

Something terrible has happened! Thieves have broken into Granny's Sweet Factory. They've made a huge mess and stolen the Secret Formula for Crackling Candy!

Granny's Sweet Factory

You rush over to the factory. The windows are dark and the machines are silent. Granny needs you to help her get the factory running again, track down the thieves and recover the special recipe.

IF YOU'RE READY FOR THE CHALLENGE, GO TO PAGE 21 TO START YOUR ADVENTURE

No. This only makes the grains of solid salt and sand smaller and more difficult to separate.

TURN TO PAGE 27 AND **TRY AGAIN**

Chalk won't have any effect on the ice.

GO BACK TO PAGE 35 AND **TRY AGAIN**

Right! Ice is the solid form of water.

The robot guard leaves. You see the golden envelope in a glass case, protected by a passcode.

ENVELOPE 3

PASSCODE PROTECTED

FIND THE MISSING STAGE OF THE WATER CYCLE

WATER VAPOUR EVAPORATES INTO CLOUDS. GO TO PAGE 16

WATER VAPOUR CONDENSES INTO CLOUDS. TURN TO PAGE 11

?

WATER FALLS AS RAIN

WATER EVAPORATES INTO THE AIR

WATER RETURNS TO THE SEA

That's right! Bases are the opposites of acids. They react with acids and neutralize them. Bases that dissolve in water are called alkalis.

The door pings open and you grab the envelope. One down... four to go!

Next door is **The Materials Testing Lab.** Peeking through the door, you see that the room is full of people. You slip inside unnoticed.

There's an exam taking place. You decide to sit down and take the test. It may lead you to more golden envelopes.

TRAINEE EXAM.
PACKAGING TESTING.
20 MINUTES REMAINING BEFORE INSPECTION.

EXAM QUESTION:

Which material would be most suitable for sweet packaging?

COTTON.
TURN TO PAGE 39

WOOD.
FLIP TO PAGE 31

PLASTIC.
HEAD TO PAGE 12

Boiling the mixture will remove the water, but the sand and salt will still be mixed together.

TURN BACK TO PAGE 36 AND **CHOOSE AGAIN**

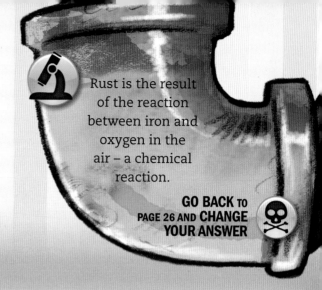

Rust is the result of the reaction between iron and oxygen in the air – a chemical reaction.

GO BACK TO PAGE 26 AND **CHANGE YOUR ANSWER**

Correct! Heat is needed to start a fire.

You grab the second golden envelope and head out to **LAB 3: Water Room.**

You try the door, but it's locked. A door panel at the side is flashing.

PASSCODE REQUIRED

FILL IN THE MISSING WORD

The movement of water around Earth is called........

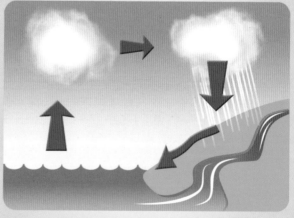

THE CONDENSATION CIRCLE.
GO TO PAGE 41

THE WATER CYCLE.
TURN OVER TO PAGE 18

The small crystals sparkle orange in the flame. That's because table salt is a chemical compound called sodium chloride, and sodium always burns with an orange flame. This is called a flame test.

Suddenly the lights go out. A power cut – just what you need!

The cold room! The ice cream will melt!

What should you do?

OPEN THE DOOR TO LET COOL AIR IN.
TURN TO PAGE 12

TURN TO PAGE 12

COVER THE ICE CREAM WITH A WARM BLANKET.
GO TO PAGE 23

GO TO PAGE 23

Marble is a hard rock, so the sweets will be hard too.

GO BACK
TO PAGE 11
AND **TRY AGAIN**

GO BACK TO PAGE 11 AND TRY AGAIN

186°C is the temperature at which sugar melts (turns to liquid). Water boils (turns to gas) at a lower temperature than this.

TURN TO PAGE 21
AND **TRY AGAIN**

TURN TO PAGE 21 AND TRY AGAIN

°C

200
150
100
50

No. Condensation is where gas turns to liquid – the opposite physical process to evaporation.

GO BACK TO PAGE 28 AND **TRY AGAIN**

Talcum powder will just cover the ice in a cloud of white. Not very helpful.

TURN BACK TO PAGE 35 AND **THINK AGAIN**

Belgian chemist Jean Joseph Etienne Lenoir produced the first gas-fired internal combustion engine in 1860.

TURN BACK TO PAGE 42 AND **TRY AGAIN**

Carbon is important because it makes up your DNA – the instructions your body uses to build and run your cells. But it isn't the most common element in the body.

TURN TO PAGE 33 AND **TRY AGAIN**

Cracked it! Condensation turns water vapour into liquid water, making clouds.

You grab the envelope and hotfoot it out of there. Only two to go! Next stop – **The Rock Lab.**

You go inside and see that the worktops are covered with rocks and soil. Beside each type of rock is a sweet designed to look and feel just like it. Maybe you'll have a little taste…

But be careful – the hard rock sweets could break your teeth. You'd better choose a soft one. So which should you try?

CHALK CHOMP

GO TO
PAGE 39

GRANITE GUZZLER

FLIP TO
PAGE 12

Marble Munchie

TURN TO
PAGE 9

Correct! Plastics are strong, waterproof and flexible. Perfect for sweet wrappers.

The examiners check everyone's answers. The five students with the best answers can stay – and you're one of them! Everyone else is told to go home.

The instructor asks a question:

> Is plastic a thermal conductor or insulator?

heat

heat

CONDUCTOR.
TURN TO PAGE 33

INSULATOR.
GO TO PAGE 22

No, you'll let in warm air too and the ice cream will melt.

TURN BACK TO PAGE TO 9 AND **THINK AGAIN**

Granite is a super-hard rock – you won't be able to bite through that.

FLIP BACK TO PAGE 11 AND **THINK AGAIN**

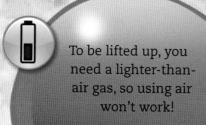

To be lifted up, you need a lighter-than-air gas, so using air won't work!

TURN BACK TO PAGE 29 AND **CHOOSE AGAIN**

No, soybeans are used to help 'glue' chocolate together.

GO BACK TO PAGE 20 AND **TRY AGAIN**

Correct! You cannot turn a cake back into its ingredients – when you mix the ingredients and bake them, you create a new substance.

You arrive at the labs. The first is **The Acid Lab.** You slip inside and come face to face with a lab technician.

LAB 1: ACIDS

I know you're new but I still expect you to turn up on time! I'm Peters — let's get on, shall we? Here's a quick test... Which of these can we safely add to our sweets?

CITRIC ACID.
GO TO PAGE 19

SULPHURIC ACID.
TURN TO PAGE 23

Correct. Tiny pores in permeable rock let water soak through. You pull out the fourth golden envelope. Only one to go! You move on to **The Chemical Lab.**

The lab is dark so you tiptoe inside. The door slams behind you and you come face to face with Kriss and Klair Krunchy, the evil bosses of the Krunch Korporation.

No, evaporation means 'turning into gas'. Water evaporates from rivers, lakes and seas when it is heated by the Sun. But as it rises higher, it cools and turns from gas back into liquid water, which forms clouds.

GO BACK TO PAGE 5 AND **TRY AGAIN**

Italian chemist Alessandro Volta invented the first battery in 1800.

TURN BACK TO PAGE 42 AND **TRY AGAIN**

That's right! You help Granny to fetch some heaters, and before long the hard chocolate is melting – turning from a solid into a liquid.

You need to make sure that the chocolate doesn't get too hot because it will burn.

Which of these should you use to test the temperature of the chocolate?

A THERMOSTAT.
GO TO PAGE 38

A THERMOMETER.
TURN TO PAGE 27

A THERMOS FLASK.
OVER TO PAGE 43

Yes, that's right! As the shavings are made of steel, they are attracted to the magnet.

As you're stirring through the sugar, you spot something gleaming – but it isn't attracted to the magnet, so it can't be metal.

You pull it out... It's a plastic button labelled Krunch Korporation – Granny's rivals! They must be behind the robbery!

IT'S TIME TO PAY THEM A VISIT ON PAGE 29

17

Don't lick the spoon – it could be extremely dangerous!

TURN TO PAGE 37 AND **TRY AGAIN**

When wood burns it reacts with oxygen in the air and creates carbon dioxide and water. Because something new has been created, this is a chemical reaction.

TURN BACK TO PAGE 26 AND **TRY AGAIN**

LAB 3: WATER ROOM

Correct. The water cycle is how water moves around the planet, on a never-ending journey from the sea to the clouds and back.

You enter the lab – it's empty but you see water in three different states. Suddenly, a robot guard whizzes over.

STEAM

ICE

WATER

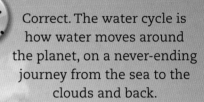

CONFIRM AUTHORIZATION. WHICH IS WATER'S SOLID STATE?

WATER.
GO TO
PAGE 20

ICE.
TURN TO
PAGE 5

STEAM.
OVER TO
PAGE 38

18

Salt *does* melt before sand – but only at 801°C. You'd need a serious oven to reach those temperatures! But melting the salt won't separate it from the sand.

GO BACK TO **PAGE 27 AND THINK AGAIN**

Correct. Citric acid is found naturally in many foods, including citrus fruits such as oranges and lemons. It is also used as an artificial flavouring in sweets, such as lemon sours and pear drops.

Actually, I'm here to take the formula to head office.

Oh. Well, the first part is over there. I hope you've remembered the passcode.

ENVELOPE 1

On the other side of the room is a glass case containing a golden envelope.

PASSCODE PROTECTED

ENTER THE OPPOSITE OF AN ACID

BASE.
GO TO PAGE 6

YEAST.
TURN TO PAGE 43

Yes – oxygen it is! Your body is mainly made up of water (H_2O). Even though there are twice as many hydrogen atoms as oxygen atoms in water, the oxygen atoms outweigh the hydrogens.

You'll never get this one! Question three: Which of these ingredients doesn't belong in chocolate?

PLANT ROOTS.
GO TO PAGE 34

SOYBEANS.
TURN TO PAGE 13

BEETLE JUICES.
OVER TO PAGE 37

 Freezing salty water might work – pure water freezes, leaving salt behind – but it's hard work. Salt lowers the freezing point of water, which is why it's spread on roads in the winter.

TURN BACK TO PAGE 41 AND TRY AGAIN

 No, water is a liquid.

GO BACK TO PAGE 18 AND THINK AGAIN

Granny takes you to the chocolate fountain – where all the ingredients are mixed together to make yummy, runny chocolate.

"The chocolate has gone hard," says Granny. *"How do we turn it back into liquid chocolate?"*

CHILL IT.
GO TO PAGE 33

HEAT IT.
TURN TO PAGE 16

 Correct! Lasers were invented by physicists, not chemists. The first laser was invented in the USA in 1953 by Charles Townes.

WELCOME STAFF MEMBER. HOW MAY I HELP YOU?

I'm here to collect the Secret Formula. Please provide me with the instructions.

ENTER THE SECURITY CLEARANCE PASSCODE.

PASSCODE PROTECTED

AT WHAT TEMPERATURE DOES WATER BOIL?

25°C.
TURN TO PAGE 28

100°C.
GO TO PAGE 40

186°C.
FLIP TO PAGE 9

Yes! Plastic doesn't let heat (or thermal energy) move through it easily, so it's an insulator.

"Let's move into the next room," the instructor says.

Just as you're about to leave with them, you spot the second golden envelope in a glass case. You hang back until everyone has left.

ENVELOPE 2

PASSCODE PROTECTED

BURNING IS AN IRREVERSIBLE CHANGE. THIS TRIANGLE SHOWS THE CONDITIONS NEEDED FOR A FIRE TO START.

But what is missing?

OXYGEN

FUEL

?

HEAT.
GO TO PAGE 8

AIR.
TURN TO PAGE 26

WOOD.
OVER TO PAGE 30

Calcium is a really important element in your bones, but it isn't the most common element in the body by a long way.

TRY AGAIN ON PAGE 33

Sulphuric acid is a strong acid and is very corrosive – it eats through anything it comes into contact with. A sulphuric acid sweet would burn straight through your tongue!

TURN BACK TO PAGE 13 AND **TRY AGAIN**

Yes, very clever! Heat travels from warm things (the air) to cold objects (the ice cream). A blanket will stop the cold air from escaping – this is called insulation. It won't stop the ice cream melting forever, but it'll buy you some time until the power comes back on!

Last of all, you tackle the sugar supplies. The intruders have poured steel shavings of all shapes and sizes into the large tank.

"How will we get them out?" asks Granny.

USING A FUNNEL. OVER TO PAGE 26

WITH A MAGNET. GO TO PAGE 17

USING A SIEVE. TURN TO PAGE 30

Granny flips a switch and the factory springs to life. To reward you for your amazing efforts – and amazing science knowledge – Granny makes you Head Chocolatier. What an ace job! Congratulations!

Funnels and filter paper are useful for separating solids from liquids, but in this case, there are two solids mixed together.

TURN BACK TO PAGE 23 AND **TRY AGAIN**

No, oxygen – which is found in air – is already present.

GO BACK TO PAGE 22 AND **TRY AGAIN**

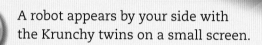

A robot appears by your side with the Krunchy twins on a small screen.

There's a canister of poisonous fluorine gas in this room. If you get just one answer wrong, it'll be released and you will be doomed. Get them all right and you may keep your life. Ha ha ha!

Question one: Which one of the following is not a chemical reaction?

A NAIL RUSTING.
TURN TO PAGE 8

SNOW MELTING.
GO TO PAGE 33

WOOD BURNING.
FLIP TO PAGE 18

A PLANT MAKING FOOD FROM SUNLIGHT.
OVER TO PAGE 41

Correct. You check the temperature of the chocolate using the thermometer. It's hot, so you'd better turn off the heaters before the chocolate burns.

Any more problems for me to solve?

The thieves have poured sand into the salt. Can you separate it?

Hmm, tricky! What do you do?

HEAT UP THE MIXTURE?
GO TO PAGE 19

POUR WATER OVER THE SAND AND SALT MIX?
TURN TO PAGE 36

WHIZ IT UP IN A MIXER?
TURN OVER TO PAGE 5

No, you can reverse this change by heating the ice to turn it back into a liquid.

GO BACK TO PAGE 40 AND **THINK AGAIN**

No, impermeable means that water won't pass through it.

GO BACK TO PAGE 31 AND **THINK AGAIN**

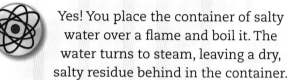 Yes! You place the container of salty water over a flame and boil it. The water turns to steam, leaving a dry, salty residue behind in the container.

"I can't believe it! What's that trickery called?" asks Granny.

"It's not trickery, it's just science! But it does have a special name," you reply.

What's it called?

 EVAPORATION.
GO TO PAGE 37

 CONDENSATION?
TURN TO PAGE 10

 Vinegar is a weak acid. It might lower the melting point of ice and make it melt more easily, but there's something that will do it much quicker...

GO BACK TO PAGE 35 AND **THINK AGAIN**

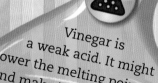

°C

Room temperature is normally about 25°C. Water is liquid at that temperature. It has to be hotter than this to boil.

TURN BACK TO PAGE 21 AND **TRY AGAIN**

You hotfoot it to the KK factory. When you arrive, you walk around the fence, looking for a way in.

You spot a large deflated balloon and some canisters – an idea hits you! It's risky, but maybe you can fly over the fence using the balloon.

Which canister contains a gas that will inflate the balloon and lift you over the fence?

CANISTER A.
GO TO PAGE 13

CANISTER B.
TURN TO PAGE 42

CANISTER C.
OVER TO PAGE 39

A
COMPRESSED AIR

B
HELIUM

C
KRYPTON

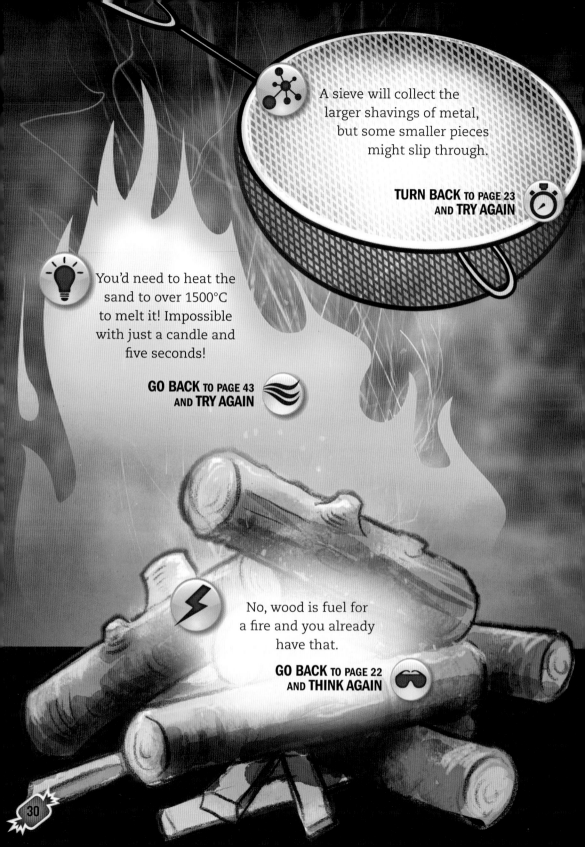

A sieve will collect the larger shavings of metal, but some smaller pieces might slip through.

TURN BACK TO PAGE 23 AND **TRY AGAIN**

You'd need to heat the sand to over 1500°C to melt it! Impossible with just a candle and five seconds!

GO BACK TO PAGE 43 AND **TRY AGAIN**

No, wood is fuel for a fire and you already have that.

GO BACK TO PAGE 22 AND **THINK AGAIN**

Wood is strong and long lasting, but if you made it thin enough for sweet wrappers, it would splinter and break apart.

GO BACK TO PAGE 7 AND **THINK AGAIN**

The particles of salt dissolved in the water are much too small for a sieve to catch.

GO BACK TO PAGE 41 AND **THINK AGAIN**

ENVELOPE 4

Correct! You reach for the envelope, but before you can grab it, a shutter slides across blocking the slot!

SANDSTONE

WATER

SECOND CODE REQUIRED. WHY DOES THE SANDSTONE LET WATER THROUGH?

IT'S PERMEABLE.
GO TO PAGE 14

IT'S IMPERMEABLE.
TURN TO PAGE 27

Yes! Water won't dissolve the sand, but it will break up and wash away the grains. Where can you get lots of water – and fast? The fire alarm! You smash the glass and the sprinkler system turns on. The sandcastle collapses. You grab the key and get out of the factory as fast as you possibly can.

The factory has been evacuated, including the drenched Krunchy twins. And the police have turned up. Granny must have called them! The Krunchy twins shout angrily at you as police officers bundle them into vans. At last the thieves will be punished!

WITH THE ENVELOPES IN YOUR POCKET, YOU SLIP AWAY, **BACK TO GRANNY ZARA'S** ON PAGE 24

That's not right. Chilling means making something colder. To turn a solid into a liquid, you need to melt it.

CHOOSE AGAIN ON PAGE 21

No, a thermal conductor, such as metal, lets heat move through it easily.

GO BACK TO PAGE 12 AND **TRY AGAIN**

Correct! Changing state (melting) is a physical change, but it's not a chemical reaction because substances don't combine or change chemically.

That was an easy one to get you started. Question two: What is the most common chemical element in the human body?

CARBON.
TURN TO PAGE 10

OXYGEN.
TURN TO PAGE 20

CALCIUM.
TURN TO PAGE 23

Before you try for the key, you notice the case with the fifth golden envelope inside. Time to finish this mission!

The box is made of ice. Just melt it and you'll get the final envelope! But there's no heat source…

There are lots of items around the room. Which item will tackle the ice?

SALT.
GO TO PAGE 43

TALCUM POWDER.
TURN TO PAGE 10

CHALK.
OVER TO PAGE 5

VINEGAR.
FLIP TO PAGE 28

You scoop the sand and salt into a container and then add water. The salt dissolves in the water, but the sand doesn't.

"How does that help? You've made a saltwater solution. How will you get the solid grains of sand out?" asks Granny.

FILTER IT.
TURN TO PAGE 41

BOIL IT.
OVER TO PAGE 8

English chemist John Walker invented the first match in 1826.

TURN BACK TO PAGE 42 AND **TRY AGAIN**

No, marble won't let water through.

GO BACK TO PAGE 39 AND **TRY AGAIN**

No, you can reverse the change by cooling the chocolate, which turns it back into a solid.

GO BACK TO PAGE 40 AND TRY AGAIN

No, tiny red beetles are crushed and used to make colourings for sweets and chocolate.

GO BACK TO PAGE 20 AND THINK AGAIN

Yes, evaporation changes a liquid into a gas. It's a great way of separating solutions.

Amazing! But how can we be sure that it's salt? It could have changed into something else!

I KNOW that it's salt, but if you want extra proof...

What do you do?

TAKE A SPOON AND TASTE IT. TURN TO PAGE 18

TOSS THE CRYSTALS INTO A FLAME. GO PAGE 9

No, steam
(or water vapour)
is a gas.

GO BACK TO PAGE 18
AND **TRY AGAIN**

No, a thermostat
is a switch that responds
to changes in temperature.
For example, the switch in
a kettle turns off when
the water inside reaches
boiling point (100°C).

TURN BACK TO PAGE 16
AND **TRY AGAIN**

Sand grains are very hard and
don't dissolve easily. You'd need
to find some super-strong acid, and that
might take a while.

THINK AGAIN
BACK ON PAGE 43

Cotton is a fabric. Although it is flexible, it's also absorbent. If the sweets get wet, they will dissolve!

GO BACK TO PAGE 7 AND **TRY AGAIN**

Krypton gas is heavier than air – a balloon filled with krypton will sink like a stone.

TURN TO PAGE 29 AND **CHOOSE AGAIN**

Chalk is a soft rock that wears away easily, so the sweet melts in your mouth. Yum!

Now you must concentrate and find the fourth envelope. You locate it in another glass case.

ENVELOPE 4

PASSCODE PROTECTED

WHICH ROCK LETS WATER PASS THROUGH IT?

SANDSTONE.
GO TO PAGE 31

MARBLE.
TURN TO PAGE 36

Correct! Water boils – turns from a liquid to a gas – at 100°C.

A message appears on the robot's touchscreen.

THE FORMULA HAS BEEN SPLIT INTO FIVE GOLDEN ENVELOPES. EACH IS LOCATED IN ONE OF THE LABS.

BUT WHERE ARE THE LABS? TO FIND THE BEST ROUTE, ANSWER THE QUESTION AND FOLLOW THE PATH.

Which one of these is an irreversible change?

MELTING CHOCOLATE

BAKING A CAKE

FREEZING JUICE TO MAKE ICE LOLLIES

BATHROOMS

RECEPTION

SHOP

MAIN OFFICE

MAIN FACTORY

STORE ROOM

STAIRS

SALES OFFICE

= SECURITY

MAIN LABORATORY

TRAINING LABORATORY

GO TO PAGE 27

GO TO PAGE 37

GO TO PAGE 13

40

There's no such thing as the condensation circle.

GO BACK TO PAGE 8 AND **TRY AGAIN**

Plants make food through a chemical reaction that uses the Sun's energy to convert carbon dioxide gas into sugary food.

TURN BACK AND **TRY AGAIN** ON PAGE 26

Yes! The saltwater solution passes through the filter paper, but the larger, undissolved pieces of sand are trapped by the filter.

"But now you just have salty water. I can't use that in my sweets. I can only use salt crystals!" cries Granny.

How do you separate the salt solution?

FREEZE IT.
TURN TO PAGE 20

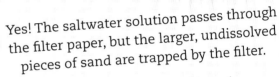

BOIL IT.
GO TO PAGE 28

STRAIN IT.
FLIP TO PAGE 31

Helium gas is less dense than air, which is why party balloons rise. You sail over the fence, landing with a bump on the other side.

Suddenly a security robot appears.

UNAUTHORIZED ACCESS! VERIFY EMPLOYEE STATUS.

WHICH ONE OF THESE OBJECTS WAS NOT INVENTED BY A CHEMIST?

Think fast before you're discovered.

BATTERY.
GO TO PAGE 16

MATCH.
OVER TO PAGE 36

LASER.
FLIP TO PAGE 21

PETROL ENGINE.
TURN TO PAGE 10

Correct. Salt lowers the melting point of ice. This makes it easier for ice to melt, so it quickly turns to water.

The box melts away and you grab the final golden envelope. Now for the key. You approach the sandcastle. The key must be somewhere inside it.

The key is hidden inside this block of sand. You have only five seconds to get it, otherwise the room will be locked forever!

Searching through the sand will take too long. How can you get the sand to disappear quickly?

MELT THE SAND?
GO TO PAGE 30

DISINTEGRATE THE SAND?
OVER TO PAGE 32

DISSOLVE THE SAND?
TURN TO PAGE 38

No, a thermos flask keeps hot liquids hot and cold liquids cold.

TURN BACK
TO PAGE 16 AND **TRY AGAIN**

No, yeast isn't the opposite of an acid. It's a special organism that is used to make bread rise.

GO BACK TO PAGE 19 AND **TRY AGAIN**

GLOSSARY

ACID
A chemical substance that is the opposite of a base. Acids neutralize bases and alkalis. Weak acids (such as vinegar and lemon) are used to flavour food, while strong acids are used as industrial chemicals and can cause burns.

ALKALI
A chemical substance that is the opposite of an acid. Alkalis neutralize acids. Unlike most bases, alkalis dissolve in water. Many cleaning products, such as bleach, contain strong alkalis that can be dangerous.

ATOM
A tiny part of matter, which forms the basic building block of a chemical element.

BASE
A chemical substance that is the opposite of an acid. Bases neutralize acids, but unlike alkalis, most bases don't dissolve in water.

BOILING POINT
The temperature at which a liquid boils and turns into a gas.

CANISTER
A container for holding gases. A gas that is kept in a metal canister is usually compressed, meaning its particles are squashed together.

CHANGING STATE
When one state of matter (solid, liquid or gas) turns into another. For example, when a solid melts, it changes state into a liquid.

CHEMICAL REACTION
When chemicals mix together to form new substances.

COMPOUND
A substance made of two or more chemical elements that have combined chemically with each other.

CONDENSATION
A change of state where a cooling gas becomes a liquid.

44

CONDUCTOR
A material that allows electricity or heat to travel through it.

CRYSTAL
A naturally occurring solid substance that has a regular shape owing to the arrangement of the atoms inside it.

ELEMENT
The simplest type of substance, made from atoms of just one kind. There are 118 known elements.

EVAPORATION
A change of state where a heated liquid turns into a gas.

FILTER
A material that is used to remove unwanted substances from liquids that pass through it.

FREEZING
A change of state where a cooling liquid becomes solid. It is also called solidification.

GAS
A state of matter in which the particles are very far from each other. Gases fill any container in which they are placed. Like liquids, they can flow but they can also be compressed (squashed). Gases are also called vapour.

IMPERMEABLE
When a material stops liquid or gases from passing through it.

INSULATOR
A material that prevents thermal energy passing through it. Insulation can be used to keep hot things warm or keep cool things chilled.

IRREVERSIBLE CHANGE
A chemical reaction where the results of the reaction cannot be converted back to the original ingredients. For example, baking a cake is an irreversible change because a cake cannot turn back into flour, eggs and sugar.

LIQUID
A state of matter in which particles are close together, but able to move and slide past each other. A liquid can be poured and it will change shape to fit a container.

HEAT
Energy that is held internally by an object. Heat flows from hot regions to cooler spots, and the temperature of an object tells you how hot it is.

MATERIAL
All substances are materials. Materials include manmade substances, such as plastic, and natural materials, such as wood.

MATTER
The 'stuff' that things are made of. Matter is made of atoms.

MELTING
A change of state where a heated solid turns to a liquid.

PARTICLE
Everything is made up of particles, far too small for the naked eye to see. For example, air is made of invisible particles of gas.

PERMEABLE
When a material allows liquid or gases to pass through.

REACTION
A chemical process where two or more substances combine to make a new substance.

RESIDUE
A substance that is left behind after a chemical process, such as a reaction, has taken place.

SOLID
A state of matter in which particles are close together, locked tightly to make a shape. A solid cannot be poured and it does not change shape to fit a container.

THERMAL
Anything to do with heat.

THERMOMETER
A piece of equipment that measures temperature.

VAPOUR
Another word for a gas. 'Vapour' is often used to refer to the gas state of a substance that is normally a liquid or solid at room temperature.

WATER CYCLE
The path that water takes around the planet. It evaporates from the oceans, condenses to form clouds, falls to the ground as rain and runs into streams and rivers, which carry it back to the oceans.

TAKING IT FURTHER

The Science Quest books are designed to motivate children to develop their Science, Technology, Engineering and Mathematics (STEM) skills. They will learn how to apply scientific know-how to the world through engaging adventure stories. For each story, readers must solve a series of scientific and technical puzzles to progress towards the exciting conclusion.

The books do not follow a page-by-page order. Instead, the reader jumps forwards and backwards through the book according to the answers given to the problems. If their answers are correct, the reader progresses to the next stage of the story; incorrect answers are fully explained before the reader is directed back to attempt the problem once again. Additional support is included in a full glossary of terms at the back of the book.

To support your child's scientific development you can:

- Read the book with your child.

- Continue reading with your child until he or she has understood how to follow the 'Go to' instructions to the next puzzle or explanation, and is flipping through the book confidently.

- Encourage your child to read on alone. Prompt your child to tell you how the story develops and what problems they have solved.

- Discuss science in everyday contexts. Cook with your child and encourage them to think of the chemistry involved.

- Play STEM-based computer games with your child and choose apps that feature science topics. These hold children's interest with colourful graphics and lively animations as they discover the way the world works.

- Most of all, make science fun!